THE STORY OF THE

CHICAGO BEARS

By Craig Ellenport

Kaleidoscope
Minneapolis, MN

BIGFOOT BOOKS

The Quest for Discovery Never Ends

This edition first published in 2021 by Kaleidoscope Publishing, Inc.

Library of Congress Control Number
2020933489

ISBN
978-1-64519-223-7 (library bound)
978-1-64519-291-6 (ebook)

FIND ME
IF YOU CAN!

Bigfoot lurks within one of the images in this book. It's up to you to find him!

TABLE OF
CONTENTS

DEE-FENSE! DEE-FENSE!

Most NFL fans like high-scoring games. They want to see their favorite team pile up points. Fans of the Chicago Bears like to see their team score, too.

Can you read the sign Bears' fans are holding up?

They like it even better when the Bears stop the other team! Chicago has always played great defense. That has helped the Bears win many NFL championships. Let's find out more about this great NFL team.

Chapter 1
Bears History

The NFL was formed in 1920. One of the first teams was the Decatur Staleys. They were coached by George Halas. In 1921, the team moved to Chicago. Halas became team owner in 1922. The first thing he did was give the team a new name: the Bears.

The Bears were one of the best teams in the early NFL. Chicago had a losing season only once in its first 25 years! The Bears won the 1933 NFL championship. They beat the New York Giants. The star of that team was Hall of Fame fullback Bronko Nagurski.

NEW NAME

When the Staleys moved, they needed a new name. In Chicago, the team played at Wrigley Field. That was home of the Chicago Cubs baseball team. A cub is a baby bear. Owner George Halas knew that football players are bigger than baseball players. So he named his team the Bears!

Halas shows his players what plays to run.

Quarterback Sid Luckman led the Bears in the 1940s. His great passing helped them win three NFL championships.

In 1963, the Bears won the NFL title again. Halas was still the team's coach! It was his sixth time atop the NFL. That was the most ever. When he retired in 1967, he had 324 **career** victories. That was also an NFL record.

Joe Marconi carries the ball for the 1963 Bears. Mike Ditka (89) is ready to help.

FUN FACT

Ditka coached the Bears from 1982 to 1992.

The Bears struggled after Halas stopped coaching. Things turned around when the Bears drafted running back Walter Payton in 1975. He quickly became one of the NFL's best. Then Mike Ditka took over as head coach in 1982. Ditka was a Hall of Fame tight end for the Bears in the 1960s. His tough style made him popular with Chicago fans. He showed the Bears how to become winners again.

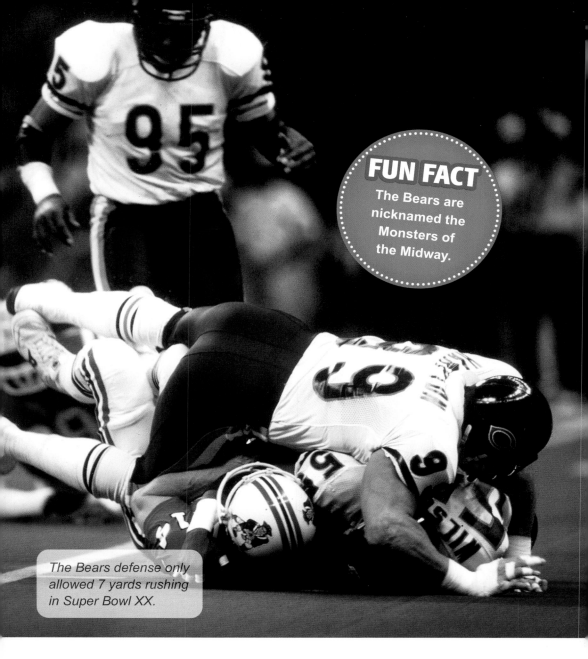

FUN FACT

The Bears are nicknamed the Monsters of the Midway.

The Bears defense only allowed 7 yards rushing in Super Bowl XX.

In 1985, the Bears had one of the best NFL seasons ever. They went 15-1. Their defense was mighty! The Bears easily won Super Bowl XX. They beat the New England Patriots 46–10.

The Bears returned to the Super Bowl in 2006. They lost to the Indianapolis Colts. Still, defense led the way again. Brian Urlacher was one of the NFL's best linebackers. He had 185 tackles in 2006.

Urlacher was great at stopping running backs.

In 2010, the Bears finished first in their division. They lost the **NFC Championship Game** against the Green Bay Packers. They struggled for the next few seasons. Before the 2018 season, they got Pro Bowl linebacker Khalil Mack from the Raiders. Mack helped Chicago have another great defense. The Bears were 12–4 and won the NFC North Division.

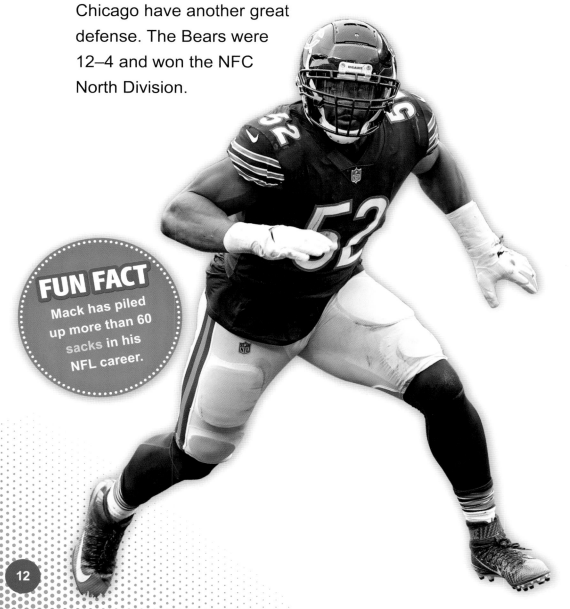

FUN FACT
Mack has piled up more than 60 sacks in his NFL career.

TIMELINE OF THE CHICAGO BEARS

1921

1921:
In the NFL's second season, Chicago wins its first championship.

1940

1940:
Chicago beats Washington in the title game. It was the most lopsided NFL game ever. The final score? 73-0!

1963

1963:
Chicago beats the New York Giants in the NFL Championship Game. It is the sixth NFL title for head coach George Halas.

1985

1985:
The Bears finish 15-1. They beat the Patriots 46-10 in Super Bowl XX.

2006

2006:
Chicago wins the NFC title. It loses Super Bowl XLI to Indianapolis.

2018

2018:
The Bears win the NFC North with a 12-4 record.

13

CHAMPIONS

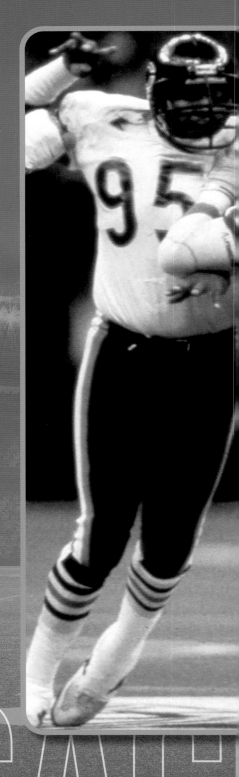

The Bears won the NFL title in 1963. They went 22 years without another one. It was worth the wait!

The 1985 Bears were almost perfect. They finished the regular season 15-1. The defense was incredible. Three of its players would later be in the Hall of Fame. The Bears held opponents to 10 points or less in 11 games. In the playoffs, they beat the New York Giants and Los Angeles Rams. The combined score was 45-0!

In Super Bowl XX, Chicago crushed the Patriots, 46-10. Time after time, Patriots runners went nowhere. They ended with a total of only seven yards! The Bears had seven sacks. They recovered four fumbles. The "D" even scored! Reggie Phillips returned an interception for a touchdown. It was one of the Super Bowl's biggest wipeouts!

Chapter 2

Bears All-Time Greats

Halas (in hat) and Luckman (42) celebrate the Bears' 1946 title.

In the 1920s, pro football wasn't as popular as college football. That started to change in 1925. The the Bears signed University of Illinois star running back Harold "Red" Grange. People from all over the country went to Bears games to see Grange play.

The Bears dominated the NFL in the 1940s. Their star quarterback was Sid Luckman. He was the league MVP in 1943. That season, Luckman set an NFL record with seven touchdown passes in one game!

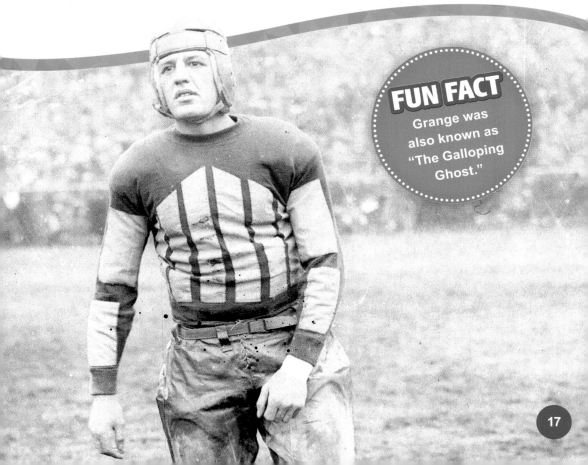

FUN FACT

Grange was also known as "The Galloping Ghost."

Running back Gale Sayers joined the Bears in 1965. He soon became one of the most exciting players in the league. With blazing speed, Sayers was always a threat to score. He ran the ball, caught passes, and returned kicks. As a **rookie**, he tied an NFL record with six touchdowns in one game!

When running back Walter Payton started playing for the Bears in 1975, he got the nickname "Sweetness." Sometimes he would dance and spin away from tacklers. Other times he would just run over them. He rushed for 16,726 yards, a career record that stood until 2002.

Sayers was known as "The Kansas Comet."

Payton shows off his high-stepping style.

Chicago has had three great middle linebackers. Each was tough, smart, and skilled. Dick Butkus joined the Bears in 1965. Opponents were afraid to run toward him! He ranks third in NFL history with 25 fumble recoveries.

Mike Singletary became a Bear in 1981. He played 12 seasons in Chicago and went to the Pro Bowl 10 years in a row. Runners never wanted to see him coming their way!

Brian Urlacher continued the tradition. Urlacher went to eight Pro Bowls. In 2005, he was the NFL Defensive Player of the Year.

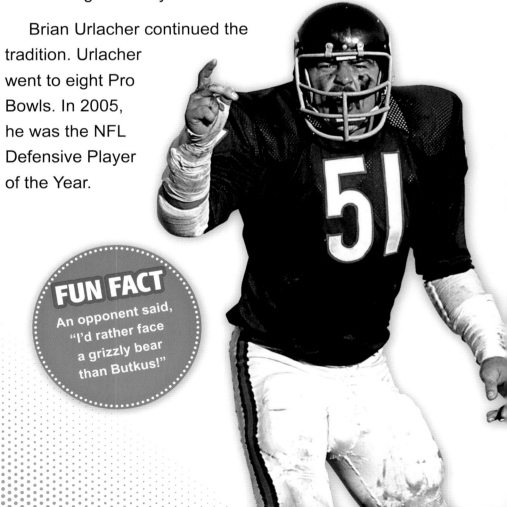

FUN FACT

An opponent said, "I'd rather face a grizzly bear than Butkus!"

BEARS

RECORDS

These players piled up the best stats in Bears history. The numbers are career records through the 2019 season.

Total TDs: Walter Payton, 125

TD Passes: Jay Cutler, 154

Passing Yards: Jay Cutler, 23,443

Rushing Yards: Walter Payton, 16,726

Receptions: Walter Payton, 492

Points: Robbie Gould, 1,207

Sacks: Richard Dent, 124.5

Chapter 3

Bears Superstars

Today's Bears keep up the team's defensive tradition. Linebacker Khalil Mack leads the way. In 2018, he had 12.5 sacks. He tied for the NFL lead by forcing six fumbles. Opponents almost always need two players to block Mack.

Cornerback Eddie Jackson has made a lot of big plays for Chicago. Jackson has five touchdowns. Three came on interception returns. Two more came on fumble returns.

Defensive tackle Akiem Hicks is the Bears' best defensive lineman. His main job is stopping the run. He has also had at least seven sacks three years in a row.

Eddie Jackson heads to the end zone with an interception.

On offense, the Bears are led by quarterback Mitchell Trubisky. He was the second overall player taken in the 2017 NFL Draft. Trubisky went to the Pro Bowl in 2018 when he passed for 3,223 yards and 24 touchdowns. Against Tampa Bay that year, he threw six touchdown passes. The Bears won the game, of course! Trubisky is also not afraid to run with the football. He already has seven rushing touchdowns in his first three seasons.

Trubisky was a star at the University of North Carolina. He threw 30 TD passes in his senior season in 2016.

Trubisky throws a pass against the Buccaneers.

The Bears have two good running backs. David Montgomery was a rookie in 2019. He led the team with 889 rushing yards. Tarik Cohen can do it all. He runs the ball, and he's very good at catching passes. He had 79 catches in 2019. His speed helps him run away from defenders!

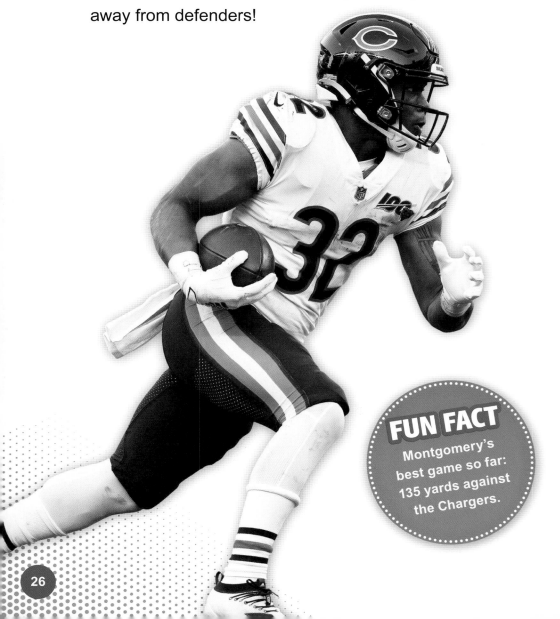

FUN FACT

Montgomery's best game so far: 135 yards against the Chargers.

Chicago's best wide receiver is Allen Robinson. He joined the Bears in 2018. Robinson had been with the Jacksonville Jaguars. In a 2018 playoff game, Robinson set a Bears record. He had 143 receiving yards against the Eagles. In 2019, Robinson had 98 catches for 1,147 yards and seven touchdowns. All three stats led the team!

Chicago wants to add to its long history of success. These are the players who will help them do it.

BEYOND
THE BOOK

After reading the book, it's time to think about what you learned. Try the following exercises to jumpstart your ideas.

RESEARCH

FIND OUT MORE. Where would you go to find out more about your favorite NFL teams and players? Check out NFL.com, of course. Each team also has its own website. What other sports information sites can you find? See if you can find other cool facts about your favorite team.

CREATE

GET ARTISTIC. Each NFL team has a logo. The Bears logo shows a large orange C. Get some art materials and try designing your own Bears logo. Or create a new team and make a logo for it. What colors would you choose? How would you draw the mascot?

DISCOVER

GO DEEP! As this book shows, the Bears were led by one man, George Halas, for decades. Read more about Halas and find out how he not only helped build the Bears, but helped build the NFL. Find out how he was as a player, too!

GROW

GET OUT AND PLAY! You don't need to be in the NFL to enjoy football. You just need a football and some friends. Play touch or tag football. Or you can hang cloth flags from your belt; grab the belt and make the "tackle." See who has the best arm to be quarterback. Who is the best receiver? Who can run the fastest? Time to play football!

RESEARCH NINJA

Visit *www.ninjaresearcher.com/2237* to learn how
to take your research skills and book report writing to the next level!

RESEARCH ·

DIGITAL LITERACY TOOLS

SEARCH LIKE A PRO
Learn about how to use search engines to find useful websites.

FACT OR FAKE?
Discover how you can tell a trusted website from an untrustworthy resource.

TEXT DETECTIVE
Explore how to zero in on the information you need most.

SHOW YOUR WORK
Research responsibly— learn how to cite sources.

WRITE ·

GET TO THE POINT
Learn how to express your main ideas.

PLAN OF ATTACK
Learn prewriting exercises and create an outline.

DOWNLOADABLE REPORT FORMS

Further Resources

BOOKS

Chandler, Matt. *Khalil Mack: Football Dominator*. Minneapolis: Capstone Press, 2020.

Storm, Marysa. *Highlights of the Chicago Bears*. Mankato, Minn.: Black Rabbit Books, 2019.

Whiting, Jim. *The Chicago Bears: NFL Today*. Mankato, Minn.: Creative Education, 2019.

WEBSITES

FACTSURFER

Factsurfer.com gives you a safe, fun way to find more information.

1. Go to www.factsurfer.com.

2. Enter "Chicago Bears" into the search box and click 🔍.

3. Select your book cover to see a list of related websites.

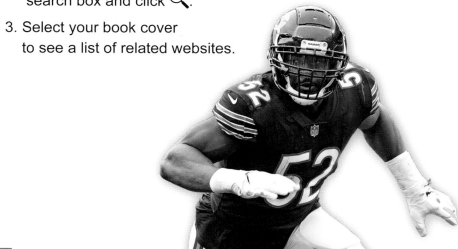

Glossary

career: the span of a person's professional life. George Halas had a 40-year career as the Bears head coach.

drafted: chosen in the NFL's annual selection of college players. With their number 1 pick in 2019, the Bears chose David Montgomery.

fumble: a ball dropped by a player; it can be recovered by either team. Khalil Mack knocked the ball out of the runner's hands for a fumble.

losing season: a year in which a sports team loses more games than it wins. With a 5–11 record, the Bears had a losing season in 2017.

NFC Championship Game: the contest that decides the winner of the National Football Conference. As the winner of the NFC Championship Game, the Bears earned a spot in the Super Bowl.

regular season: the part of the NFL season that comes before the playoffs. Chicago was 8-8 in the 2019 regular season.

rookie: a player in his or her first season of pro sports. David Montgomery's rookie season with the Bears was 2019.

sack: a tackle of the quarterback behind the line of scrimmage. The sack by Akiem Hicks sent the Packers back eight yards.

Index

PHOTO CREDITS

The images in this book are reproduced through the courtesy of:
AP Images: Vernon Biever 8; Paul Jasienski 9; Tony Tomsic 14; JDC 17.
Focus on Football: 11, 12, 18, 19, 20, 24, 26, 27. Newscom: Robin Alam/Icon SW 4; John McDonough/IconSMI 10; Brian Casells/TNS 22; Andy Reed/Icon Sportswire 24B.
Cover photo: Focus on Football.

About the Author

Craig Ellenport, a freelance writer who resides in Massapequa, New York, has written several kids books about the National Football League.